Louie's Little Lessons

A BiG KiD BED is COMiNG

written by **Liz Fletcher**   illustrated by **Greg Bishop**

Louie is an elephant hero.
He finds adventure wherever he goes.

"Whoa! Could this be a dinosaur egg?"

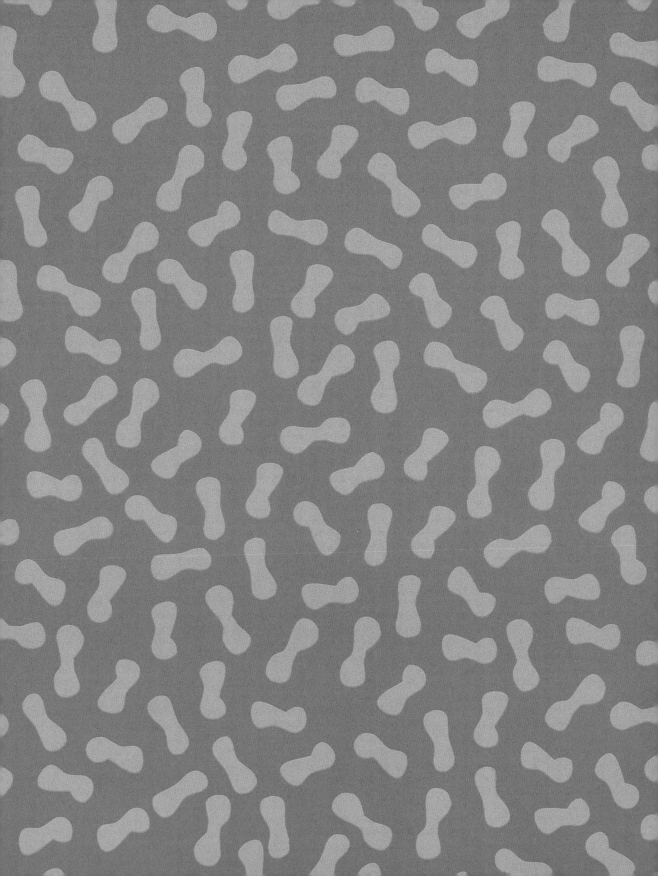

To my children, Madison and Owen, and
children everywhere. Never lose your adventurous spirit.
Run wild in your imagination. Remember to always
create, laugh, question, follow your heart, and be kind.
Reach beyond the stars—the world is yours.

© 2016 Louie's Little Lessons and Elizabeth A. Fletcher
www.louieslittlelessons.com

Books may be purchased in quantity and/or special sales by contacting the publisher, Louie's Little Lessons, at hello@louieslittlelessons.com.

Published in San Diego, California by Louie's Little Lessons. Louie's Little Lessons is a registered trademark.

Illustrations by: Greg Bishop
Interior Design by: Ron Eddy
Cover Design by: Greg Bishop and Ron Eddy
Editing by: Julie Breihan

Printed in China

ISBN: 978-0-9981936-3-2

"And there's a unicorn in polka-dot clothes."

Louie has magical powers
That let him soar across the sky.
He zooms beneath the soft, white clouds
With his cape trailing close by.

His yard is a vibrant jungle
Filled with lions, tigers, and bears.
"Shhh ... we have to be quiet.
Because look! What's that, right there?"

Louie loves being a hero,
But he's been waking up tired and weary.

He's grown too big for his little crib,
And his days are becoming less cheery.

A big-kid bed
is coming;
Louie doesn't
know what
to do.

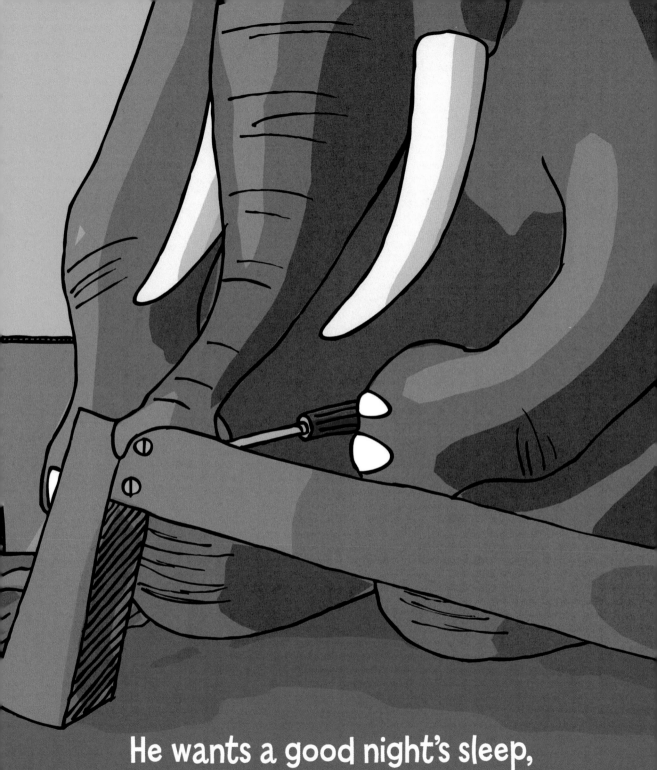

He wants a good night's sleep,
But isn't sure about trying something new.

Louie takes a deep breath
and grabs his cape.

He can feel his superpowers grow.

What am I afraid of? he thinks.
This bed looks fun. Let's go!

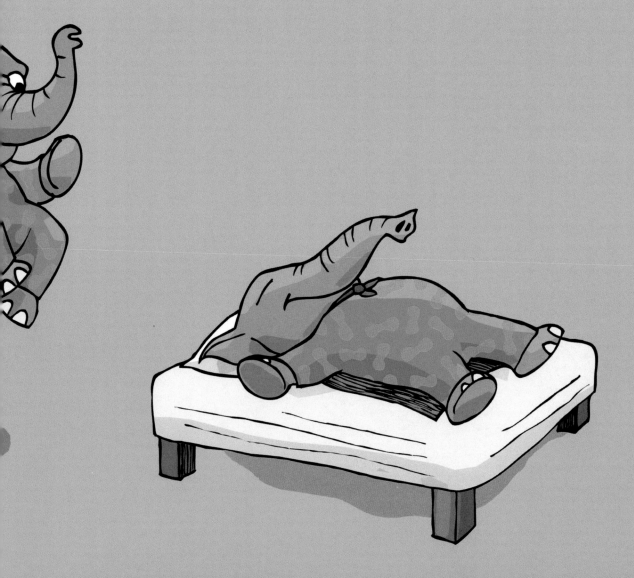

His mattress is soft and
   oh-so-big.

He can stretch, roll over,
   and play.

*I think I'll try and go
   to sleep.*

*Look! No bars are
   in my way!*

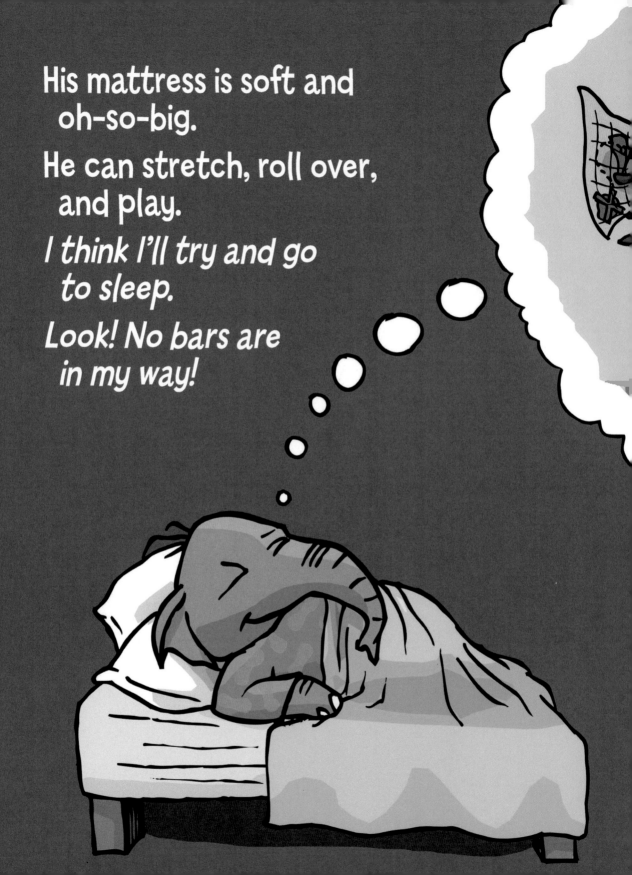

The sun is down; the moon is up.
Louie closes his eyes.
His bed turns into a pirate ship.
ARRGG! What a great surprise!

Now he is an astronaut,
Getting ready to travel to Mars.

He launches his ship
up, up, up,

Beyond the moon
and stars.

Louie's new blanket makes a perfect tent,
Protecting him from the great outdoors.
He camps among the tall, green trees.
Yippee! It's time to explore!

His pillow turns into a
magic carpet,
Flying him over the town.

The beautiful lights sparkle below.
Oh no! Don't look down!

Louie's covers keep him warm all night,
Until he sees the morning sun.

He's no longer tired or sleepy,
And his days are filled with fun.

Each night a new adventure awaits.
I just have to close my eyes!
Louie can't wait to get a good
  night's sleep
'Cause his bed is the perfect size.

Change can be exciting;
Louie's glad he tried something new.
He sure does love his big-kid bed.
And you know what? You will too!

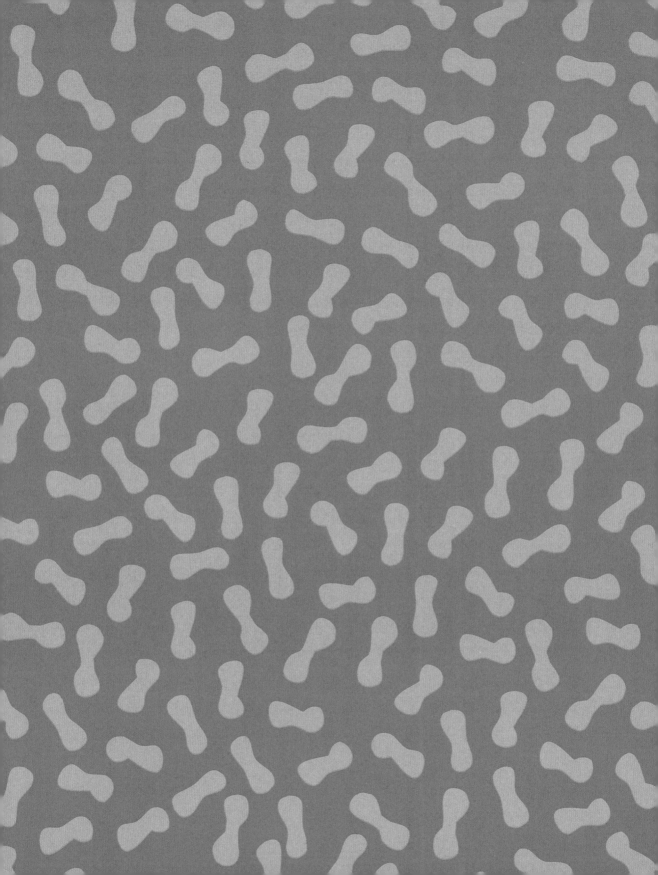

Made in the USA
San Bernardino, CA
25 June 2020